OWL'S
Question & Ans

Answers to Questions Kids Ask about

An OWL Magazine/Golden Press® Book

By the editors of OWL Magazine

wer Book #2

Dinosaurs, Horses, Snakes, Space and More

Edited by Katherine Farris
Art Direction by Nick Milton
Cover design by Elaine Groh

An OWL Magazine/Golden Press® Book
© 1983 Greey de Pencier Books, a division of Key Publishers Company, Ltd.
All rights reserved. Printed in the U.S.A. by Western Publishing Company, Inc.
OWL Magazine is a trademark of The Young Naturalist Foundation.
GOLDEN, GOLDEN® & DESIGN, and GOLDEN PRESS® are trademarks of
Western Publishing Company, Inc. No part of this book may be reproduced
or copied in any form without written permission from the publisher. Library
of Congress Catalog Card Number 83-80459.
Canadian ISBN 0-919872-83-2
U.S. ISBN 0-307-12451-7   A B C D E F G H I J

Published in Canada by Greey de Pencier Books, Toronto
Canadian Cataloguing in Publication Data
OWL's Question & Answer Book #2
(OWL Magazine/GOLDEN PRESS® Book)
Includes index.
ISBN 0-919872-83-2
1. Animals – Miscellanea – Juvenile literature.
2. Nature – Miscellanea – Juvenile literature.
I. Farris, Katherine. II. OWL (Toronto, Ont.).
QL49.A842   j570   C83-098047-4

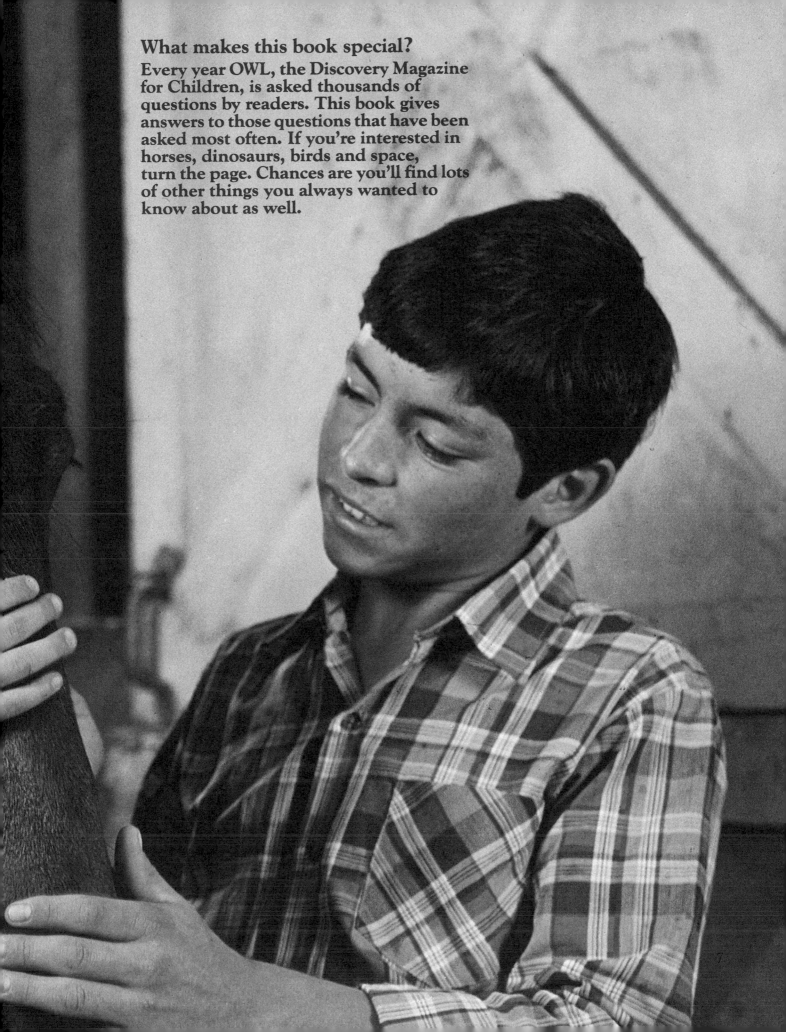

What makes this book special?
Every year OWL, the Discovery Magazine
for Children, is asked thousands of
questions by readers. This book gives
answers to those questions that have been
asked most often. If you're interested in
horses, dinosaurs, birds and space,
turn the page. Chances are you'll find lots
of other things you always wanted to
know about as well.

Why are some horses brown and others spotted?

Horses are different colors for the same reason your hair is either brown, black, red or blond. Color is inherited. Because most people prefer solid-colored horses, these tend to be bred more often. In some areas, such as the North American midwest, however, leopard-marked Appaloosas are the favorites, so you'll probably see more there.

How fast can horses run?

Very quickly! Over a short distance, quarter horses, bred for sprinting, would win the race, running about 18 m/60 feet per second. Thoroughbreds, high-spirited, streamlined horses whose ancestors are from Arabia, will run on the average 17 m/56 feet per second for three-quarters to 1½ miles.

Do horses like to race?

Horses like to run, but probably wouldn't choose to cover the distances we force them to. Because horses have a very competitive instinct, they resent being passed by other horses, and it's this that makes them try to stay ahead of the others during a race.

Why do wild horses live in herds?

Horses live in groups for protection and, some scientists believe, for companionship. A typical herd is made up of a stallion, several mares and several immature horses. In the North American west, groups of several hundred horses sometimes band together, but the average herd ranges in size from five to 40 horses.

How can you tell a wild horse from a domesticated horse?

The only true wild horses still around today are pony-like horses that stand about 127 cm/50 inches high. These Przewalskis, originally from the area around the China/Mongolia border in central Asia, now mostly live on game farms and in zoological parks. You'd know one if you saw it, not only by its size but also by its short mane, dull coloring and stocky body. Many North American horses that run free are called "wild," but they are really domesticated ones that escaped long ago as the settlers and pioneers forged across the continent.

9

How long does it take a horse to have babies?

A mare carries her foal for almost a year: 330 days. That might seem like a long time, but when the horse is finally born it's so well developed it can usually stand up within an hour or two of birth. Which is a good thing, because it needs to stand to reach its mother's underbelly for milk. Once a colt has had some milk and tested its legs – most often five or six hours after birth – it's ready to run with the herd. This was important in the wild, when herds had to keep on the move to find food and avoid predators.

How much does a horse eat?

Just to maintain itself, the average horse eats the equivalent of 35 to 40 large salad bowls full of dry hay a day. A working horse could probably pack away double that amount. Because a horse's stomach isn't big, and because it takes a lot of hay to give a horse all the nourishment it needs, horses must also eat corn, oats, barley and soybean meal for energy and protein.

How can horses sleep standing up?

Once a horse is two or three years old you'll rarely find it lying down to nap. You couldn't sleep standing up because you collapse when you are relaxed, but horses are able to lock their legs so as to stay upright. Horses sleep very little and very lightly and can rest without actually sleeping. Some horses never lie down, some do. Occasionally old horses' spines get a bit stiff, which makes it even more difficult for them to lie down and get up.

Why do horses wear shoes?

A horse's hoof is a big wraparound toenail that is tough enough for running on the ground but needs protection for traveling over roads. Horses, therefore, have their hooves trimmed regularly, and are fitted with iron shoes that are nailed in place. A horse that does a lot of work needs new shoes every six weeks or so! Being shod doesn't hurt because the shoes are nailed onto the non-living part of the horse's hooves, a part that is much like the white ends of your fingernails.

What's horse sense?

Horses seem to be able to sense problems, things that are unusual or wrong. We say people have horse sense if they can sense when "all is not well." Horse sense, for horses, is an instinct left over from their wild days. Horses are better built for escaping than fighting, so they needed to be able to sense trouble in time to avoid walking right into it.

Why do horses have tails?

A horse finds its tail pretty handy. On those days in summer when insects buzz around a horse's ears and back, the tail is an excellent fly swatter. You can often see horses standing in pairs, head to tail, swishing their tails over their own and a companion's back and head. That way they get twice the protection with half the effort.

A horse also uses its tail to show how it's feeling. A happy horse can often be seen with its tail up and over its back. If a horse is feeling out of sorts it "wrings" its tail, swishing it back and forth and around in a circle, just as people wring their hands when they're anxious.

Why do walruses lie around in crowds?

A lone walrus is an unhappy walrus. Walruses love to be close together, even though it makes for a lot of arguments. When the walruses are snuggly and warm, the blood vessels in their blubber open up and blood rushes to their skin, which is why they turn pink.

Why do pigs wallow in the mud?

Pigs don't perspire much so they wallow in mud to cool down on a hot day. First they lie on one side, then on the other, so that even their eyes and ears are covered with mud. Mud not only protects their skin from nasty pests, but also from sunburn.

Do whales spout water?

The spray you see coming from a whale's blowhole is a big breath of hot, moist air, which turns into a cloud as it cools. Mixed with that air is salt water that was trapped in a trough rimming the whale's blowhole.

Do all animals sleep?

All creatures sleep in their own way, although not necessarily the way you do. For example, horses and elephants can sleep standing up. Snakes sleep with their eyes open (because they have no eyelids) and some insects sleep by simply slowing down their body processes for a while. People once believed that sharks couldn't ever stop to sleep because they had to keep swimming in order to force water through their gills to breathe and keep afloat. Recent studies have shown that this is not necessarily true. Some sharks have been found "sleeping" on the bottom of caves along the Mexican coast.

Why do some animals have eyes in the sides of their head and others have them in front?

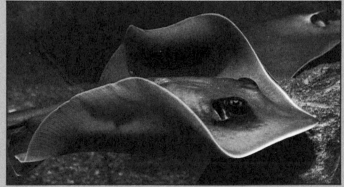

Having eyes in the sides of your head is the next best thing to having eyes in the back of your head – especially if you're a defenseless animal. With eyes on the side you can see predators trying to sneak up on you. Predators, on the other hand, are better off with eyes that face forward. To be able to judge distances, both eyes need to focus on the same object at once.

How long can a camel last without water?

A camel can run nonstop across a desert for 18 hours each day, carrying the equivalent weight of eight heavy suitcases on its back. And it can do this for over 30 days without eating or drinking. One Australian dromedary is reported to have gone for 37 days without even so much as a sip!

Why do some camels have one hump and others two?

No one really knows the answer to this question, although some scientists think it might have something to do with where camels live.

There are two main types of camels: dromedaries, which have one hump, and bactrians, which have two. The one-humped dromedary, which is the one you've probably seen in desert movies, lives in the hot, sandy countries of North Africa, the southeastern Mediterranean region, India and Australia. The two-humped bactrian lives in the deserts of Mongolia, where it gets very cold each winter. Scientists wonder if its second hump developed to store extra fat for winter.

What's the difference between caribou and reindeer?

Caribou live in Canada and reindeer live in Europe and Asia, but they both belong to the same species and are relatives of the deer family. Their noses are never red like Rudolph's, but they are furry to keep the reindeer warm.

Why do dogs pant?

Don't hush up your dog if it's panting – it's just trying to cool off. Humans get cool from the outside of their bodies by perspiring, but dogs, and other furry animals that don't sweat much, cool off from the inside by panting. Moving air quickly in and out of their lungs helps them to get rid of heat inside.

What kind of fish are jellyfish?

Jellyfish, despite their name, aren't really fish at all. They have no fins, scales or bones, not even a head. Some people think they look like a floating bag of jelly, others suggest an umbrella with streamers. But a jellyfish is simply an unusual animal made up of two layers of cells with water in between. Cells in different parts of the jellyfish have different tasks to perform. Some cells sting prey, others catch it, some digest it, others lay eggs.

What is a seashell?

A seashell is the hard, protective covering for soft-bodied animals such as oysters or clams. Clams, oysters and scallops have two shells (either side by side, or top and bottom) that open and shut. Garden snails and conches have only one shell to peek out of from time to time. Most shells are made up of three layers: an outside armor; a middle layer that gives the shell its strength and color; and an inner layer that's so smooth it is pleasant for the shell's owner to be next to.

Is a seahorse a fish?

A seahorse is a fish, but a very peculiar one. It swims upright, using the fin on its back to push it along, and has a very nimble tail that can be wrapped around seaweed almost as a monkey wraps its tail around a branch. Even a seahorse's eyes are unusual. Each is on a turret and can move independently. But the most unusual thing about seahorses is that the males look after the eggs. The mother lays up to 200 eggs in a pouch on the male's belly. He fertilizes the eggs and keeps them safe until they hatch (about four or five weeks later). Then the tiny, perfectly formed baby seahorses swim away.

Do electric eels really give off shocks? How?

Adult electric eels use their electric power to kill prey and defend themselves. They also use their electrical power like radar to "see" through murky waters, which is important because eels are virtually blind by the time they are adults.

How does it all work? Inside an eel's tail are three "batteries," one large and two small, made up of muscle and nerve endings. An eel is constantly "sensing" the water around it. The sensitivity of this electric field around the eel lets it know if something nearby is a rock, a log, or a live or dead fish. When an eel senses something swimming nearby, it sends an extra electric impulse from the large "battery" through the water. This impulse bounces back so the eel can calculate how far away the object is. Unfortunately for the object, this impulse can also kill it. A full-grown electric eel can produce enough electricity to light up as many as 10 40-watt light bulbs – probably as many as you have in your house right now.

How do oysters make pearls?

An oyster, like most mollusks, lives inside a shell lined with a smooth substance. That substance, in an oyster, is called mother of pearl and it's especially smooth. Sometimes, something such as a grain of sand will get inside the oyster's shell; when this happens, the oyster surrounds the grit spot with layers of shell material to prevent its tender body from being scratched. So that's all a pearl is: "dirt" covered with enough perfectly smooth layers of mother of pearl to make a tiny ball.

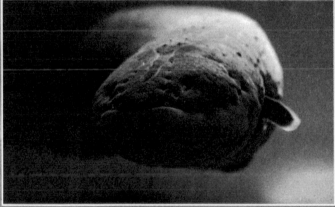

Where is a starfish's head?

Believe it or not, a starfish gets along very well without a head. Instead it has special cells all over its back that are sensitive to tastes and smells; a small, red spot on the tip of each arm that can "see" changes of light and shade; and a tiny slit in the middle of its underside, which it uses for a "mouth."

A starfish eats almost anything it encounters, including oysters, shrimps or barnacles. One meal will sometimes take as long as three days to finish. Even shells don't keep a starfish away from a meal. When a starfish finds a tasty shellfish, such as a clam, it simply wraps its arms around it, holds on tight and pulls. The clam uses its own muscles to keep its shell tightly shut, but eventually those muscles tire. When they relax, the starfish opens up the clam's shell, moves its stomach into the shell and begins to eat.

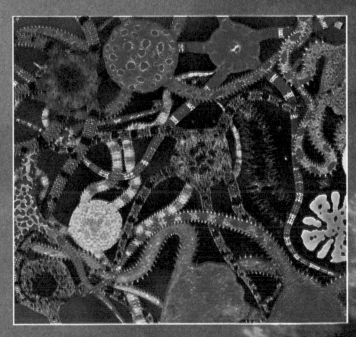

How many insects are there?

At the moment this is being written, almost 800,000 species of insects have been catalogued. But by the time you read this, that figure will be wrong, because every year scientists are finding thousands of new species. Approximately 75 to 80 percent of the animal kingdom is made up of insects (there are almost 300,000 species of beetle alone), and they've been around a long time. Insects' origins can be traced back 350 million years – which means insects were old by the time dinosaurs appeared on earth years later.

How many kinds of monkeys are there?

There are almost 200 species of primates in the world including monkeys, and related apes and prosimians (animals such as Lemurs). Almost all monkeys live in warm climates except for a few, like the Japanese macaques on the cover of this book, who keep from being chilly by lounging around in hot springs.

How fast do insects fly?

There are hundreds of thousands of different kinds of insects and they all cruise at different speeds.

If you are keen to organize an insect's Olympic team, make sure you include dragonflies. They'll whiz to the finish line at 30 kmph/18.7 mph, far ahead of the 3.2 kmph/2 mph mosquito, the 6.4 kmph/4 mph housefly or the 19 kmph/12 mph butterfly or wasp.

The fastest cruising insect ever reported is the deer botfly, a tropical insect that flies at 40 kmph/25 mph. When trying to avoid an enemy, most insects can put on a spurt. If it's threatened, a dragonfly can double its speed but not for long.

How old is the oldest living tree?

California is home to the world's oldest living single tree, a 4,600-year-old bristling pine. There was another bristlecone 300 years older, but it was cut down in 1964. Both of those trees were alive when the pyramids of Egypt were being built and scientists think that the one that is still standing could live 1,000 years longer.

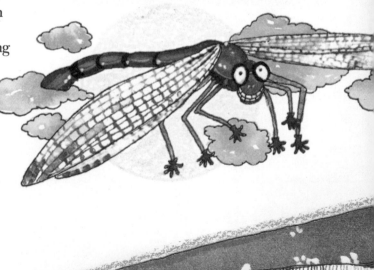

What's the fastest fish?

Don't ever try to race a sailfish – it can swim more than 96 kmph/60 mph – that's as fast as many a highway speed limit.

What's the heaviest bird that flies?

If you've ever tried to get aloft by flapping your arms, you'll be able to imagine what the Kori bustard of East Africa has to do to fly. It weighs about as much as a nine-year-old human, so perhaps it's no surprise that even though it has wings twice as long as your arms, it only manages to get as high as 60-91 m/ 200-300 feet above the ground.

How many kinds of birds are there?

There are more than 8,600 species of birds. Some birds, such as the barnswallow, have many relatives around the world within their species, while others, such as the kiwi, have just a few in one area. There are tens of millions of individual birds that live on earth today and they all have two things in common: they all lay eggs and they all have feathers.

What's the biggest turtle in the world?

Turtles that live in the sea are the largest and heaviest. Imagine paddling into a leatherback. Its flippers span 3.6 m/12 feet, it has a shell bigger than an average kitchen table and it weighs almost as much as a subcompact car.

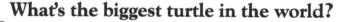

What's the biggest animal on earth?

The blue whale, as long as two buses end to end, is the biggest animal on earth and a good bet for the animal with the largest lungs too. Imagine what would happen if blue whales could sneeze!

What do snakes eat?

Snakes eat all sorts of things. Yellow rat snakes, which live in trees, eat birds, birds' eggs and small mammals they find on the ground. Swamp-dwelling snakes, such as the South American anaconda, snack mostly on fish, but can gobble up a sheep that ventures too close to the water's edge. Some snakes, such as the king snake, even eat poisonous snakes. They can do this because they are immune to other snakes' venom.

Snakes often eat prey larger than themselves. This isn't because their appetites are bigger than their stomachs. Their jaws are held together by an elastic ligament that can stretch and stretch to cover their prey the same way a sock slides over a foot.

When a snake eats an egg, which it loves to do, it first curls around it so that the egg won't roll away. Then the snake opens its jaws and moves the egg into its throat, where sharp spines pierce it and neck muscles squeeze it until it collapses. Once the egg is in its stomach, the snake spits out the empty eggshell. Large snakes, such as constrictors and anacondas, eat pigs in the same way, although they usually will only eat dead pigs. When finished, they spit out the big bones.

Why do snakes shed their skin?

As a snake grows, its skin gets tighter and tighter. To rid itself of its uncomfortably tight girdle, the snake grows a new skin underneath and, when it's ready, slithers out of the old. Younger snakes may shed their skins three or more times a year, whereas older snakes, once they have stopped growing, rarely shed their skins at all.

What is venom? What does it do to people?

There are two kinds of venom, and both are very harmful. One, called neurotoxin, affects a victim's nervous system. Any creatures bitten by cobras or seasnakes get a dose of neurotoxin. This acts on their central nervous system and prevents messages from being sent from their brains to various parts of their bodies. Because their lungs are no longer being told to breathe, the victims die of suffocation.

The other kind of venom, called hemotoxin, works on the bloodstream, causing the blood to coagulate and stop flowing.

Why do snakes stick out their tongues? Do they bite with them?

Forget everything you know about tongues when you think about snakes. A snake isn't being rude when it sticks out its tongue, nor is it licking or tasting. So what good is the tongue? A snake darts its tongue in and out through a hole in its upper jaw to pick up particles in the air to take them to two small cavities in the roof of the snake's mouth. From here, the scent of the particles wafts up to the snake's Jacobson's organ which is above the roof of its mouth. The Jacobson's organ helps the snake know what it is smelling.

What was the smallest dinosaur?

The smallest dinosaur, Compsognathus, was no bigger than a chicken. The Compsognathus appeared about the same time as the first birds, more than 200 million years ago, and scientists think it might even have looked a bit like a wingless, featherless bird. It had a thin, bird-shaped body and walked on chickenlike hind feet. Although the Compsognathus was tiny compared to most of its relatives, sharp, flesh-ripping teeth and three-clawed front "arms" made it a dangerous predator of many smaller creatures.

How do we know what dinosaurs looked like?

Paleontologists, just like detectives, have pieced together dinosaurs' bones and have studied skin impressions in rocks. Many museums have special exhibits featuring dinosaurs, but scientists have recently discovered that some dinosaur bones have been put together incorrectly. Watch for changes in exhibits.

What dinosaur was the largest?

Diplodocus was the longest, about the length of two modern buses. But it wasn't as heavy as Brachiosaurus, which was shorter and about as high as a bus on end. Brachiosaurus was the "heavy," weighing about the same as nine full-grown elephants.

Were dinosaurs brightly colored?

The color of an animal fades very quickly after it dies, so it is impossible to tell from the remains that have been found buried in rocks what colors dinosaurs were.

How did dinosaurs have babies?

Because of the egg shells scientists have found, it is believed that dinosaurs laid eggs in shallow holes in the warm sand, then covered them and left them to hatch. Baby dinosaurs crawled out, just as young turtles and crocodiles do today.

How did dinosaurs die?

Something happened 65 million years ago that destroyed three-quarters of all life on earth – including dinosaurs. Was it a sudden catastrophe, or was it a long, slow process? Whatever it was, only plants, mouselike animals, birds and insects survived.

This riddle has long fascinated scientists. Perhaps sun flares or an exploding star bathed the earth in deadly radiation. Or maybe there was massive volcanic activity that produced so much dust that sunlight was blocked off. Or maybe the earth passed through a dust cloud, causing world temperatures to drop, or perhaps several events combined to bring about the mass extinction.

Most scientists now believe that most of the world's plants and animals died out slowly as a result of a gradual change in climate. They say that if part of each year started to get very cold, only those creatures able to adapt – for example, warm-blooded animals with fur or feathers for insulation – could have survived. Dinosaurs had neither fur nor feathers, so gradually they perished.

Did dinosaurs make noises?

No one really knows if dinosaurs made noises, but it is thought that the hollow crests on the heads of a family of dinosaurs called hadrosaurs contained an air passage from nose to throat where loud sounds were made. But these air passages could also have been used to improve the dinosaurs' sense of smell.

Did cavemen kill and eat dinosaurs?

Cavemen did not have anything to do with dinosaurs because the last one disappeared 60 million years before the first human appeared on earth. Dinosaurs, some of which were the largest animals ever to exist on earth, lived during what is called the Mesozoic era, which lasted from about 225 to 65 million years ago.

Is a duck-billed platypus a duck or a mammal?

A duck-billed platypus (also called a duckbill, watermole or duckmole) has hair and feeds its babies milk and is therefore classified as a mammal. But a platypus is a most unusual mammal: it lays eggs and the male can squirt venom from its hind ankles for defense and to subdue a female during mating.

The platypus, while not a duck, is quite ducklike. It has a wide, rubbery bill, just right for rooting out the crayfish, shrimps, worms, mollusks and other small water animals that it dearly loves to eat. Also, like a duck, the platypus lives both in water and on land. Its webbed feet help it swim easily and its hind feet serve as rudders. On land it pulls back the webbing on its forefeet so it can burrow and claw easily.

Where do platypuses live?

You can find platypuses in fresh-water streams and lakes in southeastern Australia and Tasmania. They live in long (4.5-9 m/15-30 foot) burrows that feature one entrance on land and one in the water, and, for defense, mud and earth blockades built at intervals between the two entrances.

One end of a platypus's burrow is a nesting chamber lined with wet grass and leaves carried there by the female on her tail. The female lays one to three somewhat leathery eggs, which take about 10 to 12 days to hatch. The female rarely leaves her chamber while caring for her eggs, but when she does she rebuilds the blockades – rather like you locking the door when you go out.

How does a platypus feed its young?

Unlike other mammals, a female platypus has no teats. Her babies lap up milk that flows from milk-producing slits in her abdomen. Young platypuses are born hairless and blind and their eyes don't open for nearly 11 weeks. When born, platypuses have teeth, but these are later replaced by horny ridges that become a bill. Babies are weaned at four months and become mature at about 2½ years. All in all, platypuses live about ten years.

How can a platypus see underwater?

When a platypus dives underwater, its eyes and the inner ears, which are in a furrow on either side of its head, are closed. This means that the platypus is blind and deaf when underwater. But that doesn't really matter, because it relies on its bill to root out its food.

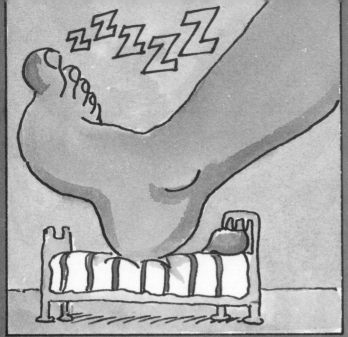

Why does your foot fall asleep when you sit for too long?

Remaining in one position for a long time can prevent your blood from circulating. For example, sometimes a blood vessel is pinched closed when you sit cross-legged. This cuts off the supply of blood to your leg and foot, making muscles and nerves there feel numb. When you get up or shake a foot that's "asleep," you get a tingly feeling because the blood starts to flow again, "waking up" the nerves and muscles.

Why do people yawn?

Suppose you're in a boring class and you start to nod off. All of a sudden – yawn! It seems a silly thing to do, and, indeed, scientists don't really know what causes yawns or what effect they have.

Yawning may be your body's way of taking in a quick "oxygen snack" when you are tired and your brain needs some oxygen in a hurry. Unfortunately, this snack doesn't last long; you may be fast asleep before the class is over.

What is a hiccup?

Since it's hard to get hiccups to happen in a lab, scientists aren't completely sure what they are. Some believe that the problem is caused by the glotus, which is a piece of flesh at the top of your voice box that flaps up and down. Designed to keep things such as water, saliva and food from sliding down into your windpipe, the movement of the glotus is supposed to keep rhythm with your breathing. Sometimes, though, the glotus gets out of rhythm and this, they think, is what gives you hiccups. Why the glotus gets out of rhythm has scientists baffled. Some believe it's caused by a small problem in the control center of the brain – when the brain skips a beat it causes your glotus to get out of rhythm too.

What is a sixth sense?

Have you and a friend had exactly the same thought at the same moment? Some people think it's your sixth sense at work. Most of our information about the world comes from our five senses: sight, hearing, touch, taste and smell. Those who believe we also have a sixth sense claim that this special sense allows us to read minds, "look" into the future and even dream things before they happen. Many scientists aren't convinced that we really have a sixth sense. They think it's just coincidence rather than some mysterious mental power at work. But many others believe that people aren't able to understand how we respond to certain kinds of extrasensory or "psychic" information and that therefore it is best to remain open-minded about the possibility of a "sixth sense."

Why do people snore?

When people sleep some of their nose and throat muscles relax and droop slightly. Sometimes they block the airways from the lungs and create turbulent whirlpools of air, which behave sort of like air in a pipe organ. When people snore, what you hear is this turbulent air flow and, sometimes, the sound of the throat muscles gently flapping as well.

What makes the sound when you snap your fingers?

As you snap your fingers, your middle finger suddenly slips off your thumb and, a split second later, strikes the fleshy pad at the base of your thumb. The snap is caused by skin hitting skin and by air erupting out from between your finger and thumb. These sudden motions send tiny molecules of air crashing into one another. This sets up a chain reaction of molecule collisions – a bit like dominoes falling down in a row. When the air molecules in your ear crash against your ear drums, your brain hears the collision as a "*snap*".

Why do people get cranky?

Your body is an amazing machine – and, like all machines, it needs regular maintenance. Every time you go to sleep, it's as if thousands of tiny mechanics leap into action all over your body, mending worn tissues, fixing the frayed connections between nerve endings, and more – all to get you ready for the next day. When you feel tired, your body is telling you, "C'mon, it's time for some maintenance, please." To make certain that you've understood the message – and that everyone else understands too – your brain makes you feel short tempered and cross. So when your mom says, "Go to bed, you're cranky," she's got your message.

Why do some people go bald?

Alas, there isn't a very satisfactory answer to this question. Some scientists believe you inherit baldness from your parents. Others believe some people's changing body chemistry causes them to go bald, while still others think that if your blood circulation is poor, and thus your scalp doesn't get enough nourishment, your hair falls out. Sometimes loss of hair is simply caused by poor hair care. One fact is certain: men are much more likely to go bald than women.

Why is some hair straight while other hair is curly?

The curliness or straightness of your hair depends on its sensitivity to the effects of humidity and heat. If you cut a straight hair in half crosswise and look at it under a microscope, you'll see that it is perfectly circular, while a curly hair is oval. On humid days some hair changes shape slightly, which is why you might be one of those people whose hair is curly during the humid days of summer but straight during the winter.

Why are some people left-handed and others right-handed?

Different areas of your brain control different parts of your body. The right side of your brain controls the left side of your body and the left side controls the right. Since there's a limited amount of space in your brain and many actions, such as writing, require only one hand, your brain gears up one way or the other.

More people's brains tell them to be right-handed, but either is quite normal. How is it decided whether you'll be left- or right-handed? Here are two of many ideas: Some scientists believe this is something you inherit from a parent or grandparent; others believe that newborn children can use either hand just as well and it's chance that causes them to start using one or the other.

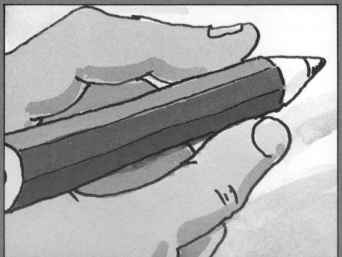

How does an inoculation keep you from getting measles?

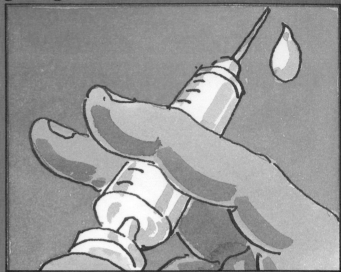

When a doctor gives you a shot for measles, he or she is actually giving you a very mild infection of the measles. Usually this infection is so weak you don't even notice it, but your body does. It immediately begins to manufacture disease-fighters called antibodies. Once in your body, these antidisease antibodies stay there ready to fight off a real attack of measles if it ever comes along.

Why do feet smell?

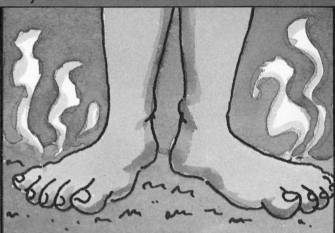

The skin on your feet, like the rest of your skin, is covered with tiny sweat glands that are there to help you keep cool. These sweat glands ooze a liquid that is mostly water, but also contains some salt and a chemical called urea. It's the urea that causes the sweat to smell. Your feet don't sweat any more than your hands or armpits do, but because feet are usually wrapped up in socks and shoes most of the time, the sweat has nowhere to escape. It just collects all day, and when you take your shoes off – whew! P.S.: If you don't wash your feet often, bacteria start to grow on them and make them twice as whiffy.

Why does the sound of fingernails scratching on a blackboard bother us?

No one knows for sure why most of us find this screech so unpleasant, but here's one theory. The sound produced by scratching fingernails on a blackboard is very high pitched – high enough to make some people's ears hurt. And because it sounds like a shriek, our brains might unconsciously think it's also a threatening sound. The combination of pain and what we think is a danger signal is enough to make us jump when fingernails and blackboard connect.

How do you feel things?

All along the surface of your skin are tiny nerve ends. When your skin touches something gently, some of the nerve ends react, allowing you to determine the shape and texture of the object you've touched. Other nerve ends are pain receptors that, when injured or touched by something hot or cold, send messages about these things to your brain. Different areas of your body have different numbers of nerves, and because of this, your brain can be fooled.

For example, try this trick on a friend: press the ends of two pencils fairly close together on your friend's back. See if your friend can guess how many pencils you used. The answer will probably be one.

Why? Because the nerves that sense touch on your back are few and far apart, they can't send precise messages to your brain. See what happens when you try the trick on the pad of a friend's thumb. Was he or she fooled?

How much blood do we have in our body? If we give blood away, how do we get it back?

If you were to step on the scales, then drain off all the water in your body, you'd be taking away 70 percent of your weight. Of that 70 percent only 15 percent is actually blood. Put another way, a 68 kg/150 pound man has 5½ l/186 ounces of blood in his body. So 450 cc/15.2 ounces (which is all we donate at a time) is really very little in terms of the body's entire blood content.

Your body is like a factory that is always running smoothly. When it realizes that there's a sudden shortage of blood, this "factory" speeds up the work process because to get blood "back," your body has to make it. Your blood is made up of a straw-colored liquid called plasma, red cells, white cells and platelets. Once you've given blood, fluids already in your body and those you drink after donating quickly help to form new plasma. To replace red and white cells, many different areas of the body go on overtime. Red cells are primarily replaced by bone marrow; white cells are replaced from many sources, including the lymph glands, as well as bone marrow; and the liver manufactures the proteins, albumins and globulins we need. The entire refuelling job from the loss of 450 cc/15.2 ounces of blood takes about two weeks.

Why are all babies born with blue eyes?

All babies – even animal babies – are born with pale, colorless eyes, but their irises look blue because of the way the light reflects off them. Eye colors, like the colors in your paintbox, are made by a substance called "pigment." Babies begin to produce pigment when they're born, but it takes a few days or weeks before there's enough to make a definite color show up in the eyes.

How can the moon shine when it's dark?

The moon shines all the time, even during the day, but you can see it better at night just as a lamp seems brighter at night than at noon. Why does the moon shine nonstop like this? It's like a gigantic mirror in the sky, reflecting the sun's light back to earth.

Why does the moon look larger when it's close to the horizon?

Before thinking about that, look at this drawing and decide which toy soldier looks the largest. Most people would say the one on the right. Because other things in the picture make that soldier look farther away, your brain thinks he's taller than the others. But measure the soldiers and you'll find they're exactly the same size. You were fooled.

When you can see the moon at the same time as other things – such as buildings, mountains, trees and so on – it looks larger for the same reason. But if you hold up your little finger at arm's length, you'll find that the tip of it covers the moon whether it's low on the horizon or high

What is the moon made of?

When the astronauts traveled to the moon, they gathered rocks and dirt from the surface and brought the samples back to earth in special boxes. Scientists who have studied this material say that the moon is made mostly of material similar to basalt, the most common type of rock we have on earth. But the basalt on the moon has been mostly smashed into gravellike rubble by meteorites crashing into the moon for millions of years.

Why do stars fall?

If you watch carefully on a dark night when there are lots of stars in the sky, every once in a while you may see what looks like a star falling quickly. Then it disappears. Although some people call this phenomenon a falling star or a shooting star, it isn't a star at all. What "fell" was a peanut-sized meteor – a bit of rubble sailing around in outer space. Meteors, which are out there by the trillion, travel 100 times faster than a jet aircraft. If they happen to come close to the earth, they rub against atoms in our atmosphere, which causes so much heat that the meteors usually burn up before they hit the ground.

Why do people float in outer space?

If you have ever bounced on a trampoline, or felt a sinking feeling in your stomach when flying in an airplane during turbulence, you have some idea of what it feels like to be floating in outer space. At the highest point of your bounce, you get a strange feeling of weightlessness, as if you are floating.

Rocketships that carry astronauts into space work like a trampoline. They are powerful enough to keep you traveling at a speed that escapes the force of the earth's gravity. Thus the astronauts, and everything else not anchored down in the ship, "floats" around. How fast a spaceship must be going for its astronauts to escape from the earth's gravity and feel weightless is determined by how far out the craft is in space – and thus how far it is from the effect of the earth's pull. If you take off from other planets or the moon, which also have gravity that pulls things toward them, your spaceship has to go fast enough to counteract their gravitational pull also.

There is a mid-point between the earth and the moon where neither's gravity affects the spaceship, so even if the craft were stopped, the astronauts would still feel weightless. It's only when the rocket's engines are fired that the astronauts are pushed back against their chairs, just as you are when your plane takes off.

If there's no air in space, what is there?

Higher than about 32 km/20 miles above the ground, there's hardly any air, and far out in space there isn't any at all. That's why it's called space – it's almost completely empty. Special instruments on spacecraft have found a few specks of dust, as well as some atoms thrown off the sun by solar flares and some fast-moving particles called cosmic rays. But there are so few of these that you wouldn't notice them if you were right out there in space with them. In fact, all you would see is blackness – and thousands of stars.

Why do some flowers close up at night?

Scientists aren't sure why flowers close at night. Plants that grow straight, such as tulips, probably close at night to protect their delicate inner parts from rain and cold. Whatever the reason, once a flower begins to close at night, it's almost impossible to stop it. The four o'clock flower, for example, shuts up tight late every afternoon and won't open again until early the next morning.

Why do plants lean towards light?

Plants are always moving, although usually they do it so slowly you can't see. Plants move toward sunlight because the more light they get, the more food they can make for themselves and the better they'll grow. To make your plants grow straight, turn their pots a little every day.

Do all plants need sunlight?

About one out of ten plants in the world can get along very well without sunlight. Those that need the sun use it to help them make food. Those that don't need sun feed on other plants or even animals. These plants are called fungi – better known as molds, yeasts and, of course, mushrooms. Food for most mushrooms is rotting plants or animals, so they're part of nature's built-in janitor service.

Why do plants have seeds?

Most, but not all, plants have seeds that are simply baby plants that can eventually grow into big plants. Each seed has two parts: an embryo, which contains a young root that will grow downward to find water and a shoot that will grow up to the light and air; and a storage area, which provides the embryo with food.

Seeds can be so small they look like dust. Or they can be like double coconut seeds, too big to hold in your hand! Most plants that form seeds produce a large number of them because only a few will live. Some seeds die before they find the right spot to grow, others become food for animals.

Why do tree stumps have rings?

For each year of a tree's life you'll see one light and one dark band on the stump, together called an annual ring. Each light-colored ring shows how much the tree has grown each spring and each dark-colored ring shows the late summer and fall growth. By counting the dark rings on a tree stump you can tell exactly how old a tree was when it was cut down. Start counting at the oldest part of the tree: the center.

Trees that have rings are usually found in temperate climates in which plants grow quickly in the spring and early summer and slowly in the late summer and autumn. In the tropics many trees don't have rings. Since it's almost always warm and wet in these areas, trees grow evenly throughout the year.

How can owls hunt at night?

Perhaps the most amazing thing about an owl is that it could probably hunt blindfolded, zeroing in on its prey by sound alone. Tucked behind its flat face feathers are big, super-sensitive ears that can tune in on the tiniest squeak or rustle. The owl also has excellent eyes, but most hunt at night because that's when prey – mice, rats and moles – come out in search of food.

Do hummingbirds really hum?

Hummingbirds have a very special way of beating their wings – up to 50 times a second in a figure-eight pattern. When you look at a hummingbird in flight all you can see is a blur – but you can hear the wings humming – hence the name.

Why do chickens have white and dark meat?

Dark meat is made up of muscles that have to be stronger than the other muscles in the bird's body because they have so much work to do. Chickens, for example, only have dark meat on their legs, because it's these muscles that are used for walking. Ducks that fly and swim have dark meat all over their bodies because both their chest and leg muscles must work hard. The dark color comes from a special pigment, called myoglobin, that carries oxygen to the muscles for fuel. White meat is made up of muscles that are only used for sudden spurts of energy (for instance, when a chicken flaps its wings). These muscles can get by without so much oxygen. Instead they burn up sugar that's stored in the body. The sugar is used up very quickly, which is why a chicken can't flap for long.

34

How can eagles glide?

When you see an eagle soaring effortlessly in the sky, it's hitching a ride on the hot air currents called thermals that the sun creates. This kind of flying is called thermal soaring. People in gliders and hang gliders soar in the same way.

Why do pelicans have such big bills?

A pelican finds its bill useful for two reasons. It can use it to scoop up the equivalent of six goldfish bowls of water full of little fish. Then when it's time for the young to eat, the parent's bill can be used as a big bowl. The young stick their head inside and feed.

Can a parrot really talk?

Despite the fact that some people enter their parrots in talking contests (the world's record holder has talked for 11 years nonstop), Polly doesn't really know what she means when she tells you to "go jump in the lake." A parrot makes parrotlike squawks, just as other birds make birdlike sounds. But what a parrot *can* do well is mimic sounds that aren't naturally birdlike – especially human voices.

What's an eggshell made of?

An eggshell is made of layer upon layer of chalklike calcium salts. Because a shell is layered, oxygen and moisture can pass through these layers into the egg, and carbon dioxide and other wastes can escape. Birds that nest near the water must be very careful not to let their eggs fall in. If the eggs sat in water for a long time so much water would pass through the shell that the incubating chicks would drown.

Inside an eggshell is an air space at the larger end. Next is the egg white, called albumen, wrapped in a very thin membrane, which acts as a cushion around the yellow yolk, and the small ovum – the special female reproductive cell – that floats on top of the yolk. The yolk and the ovum don't roll around in the egg because they are held in position by twisted strands of albumen, called the chalaza, that are on either side of the yolk. When birds are incubating their eggs, they will often turn them so that the embryo doesn't stick to the membrane protecting it and become malformed.

To identify the eggs on these pages, see the chart on page 44.

How long does it take for birds' eggs to hatch?

The time it takes an egg to hatch depends on the species of bird, the egg size and the air temperature. Those birds that spend only a short time in the egg usually will need more parental care when hatched. Baby songbirds, blind, naked and helpless when hatched, are in their eggs for a mere 10 to 14 days.

Chickens, ducks and game birds incubate their eggs for three weeks or longer, so their babies are usually covered with warm down when they hatch. They're usually able to follow their parents almost immediately and to pick up food for themselves. The bird that incubates its eggs the longest is the royal albatross – about 81 days. There are few rules in nature: albatross babies are helpless when they hatch, and they can't fly or hunt for food until they're nearly nine months old.

Why are birds' eggs oval?

There's a very practical reason for certain birds to lay oval eggs. Oval eggs fit well together in a nest and this helps to keep them warm. And even if a nest is no more than a few twigs on a rocky ledge, the eggs will always roll downhill toward the middle.

Different species of birds lay differently shaped eggs. Noddy birds' eggs, for example, are flattened, which helps to keep them from falling off the branches on which they are laid!

Is it true that a porcupine can shoot its quills?

An adult porcupine has about 30,000 light, hollow quills, which grow all over its body except on its face, legs, belly and the underside of its tail. On the quills' shafts are tiny barbs that stick into things, making them difficult to pull out. While a porcupine does not shoot its quills, it does use them as a weapon. When a porcupine is mad or frightened, it turns its back on its enemy, makes its quills stand on end and shakes its tail. Often the attacker will be hit by the tail and some quills will stick in its body.

A porcupine's quills are not poisonous, but they may slowly work their way through the attacker's body, possibly causing infection. The porcupine, meanwhile, ambles on its way, growing new quills to replace the old.

Is it true that you get warts if you touch a toad?

You won't get warts if you touch a toad. Warts on human skin aren't caused by touching something; instead, they are caused by a virus that you catch. Although a toad's skin might look warty – and although its bumps are actually called "warts" – touching a toad won't make your skin look that way.

Nevertheless, toads do not make great playmates. For protection, they ooze out a poisonous liquid from two glands behind their eyes. If you get any of this on your hands and then touch your eyes or mouth, you'll feel a burning sensation. Needless to say, this is effective protection for toads. While a predator may eat one toad, the sensation is so awful it will probably never eat another!

Is a ladybug good luck? If so, why does the poem say it should fly away home?

Ladybugs are considered to be good luck by farmers because they eat pests such as plant lice (aphids), mealybugs and other insects that destroy farmers' plants and crops.

The chant about ladybugs came from Germany, where, after a farmer harvested a field of hops, it was customary to burn the vines to destroy pests and prepare the field for the next planting. Since baby ladybugs are wingless and therefore unable to fly, the farmers hoped the adults would whisk them away somehow to safety.

Is it true that ostriches hide their heads in the sand?

When a male ostrich sits on its nest, it sometimes lays its head flat on the sand, and since its head and long neck are sand colored, they almost disappear from sight. What's left sticking up – the ostrich's lovely feathery behind – looks so much like a bush that even the smartest predator is fooled.

Is it true that you can hear the sea in a seashell?

When you put a seashell up to your ear, you can hear a muffled roar that sounds just like the sea. If you cup your hand around your ear, you'll hear almost the same sound. The shape of the shell, or your cupped hand, traps the sound waves in the air and causes them to break up. What sounds like the rhythm of the sea pounding on the shore is really just a jumble of sounds getting smashed up. The best-shaped shell for special sound effects is the conch.

Is it true that a camel stores water in its hump?

Years ago people believed that because the camel could survive for days in the desert without drinking, its hump must contain water. We now know that this isn't so. The camel's hump contains fat – it's an energy storage tank for use when food is scarce.

How can a fly walk upside-down on the ceiling and not fall off?

Look at this fly's middle foot. It's wide and has two big hooks and soft, rounded pads. Now imagine you're this fly. You weigh practically nothing at all, so you're like an astronaut in space. Because gravity isn't pulling you down and you have six hooked feet that can grab all the craters and cracks in the ceiling, you are well anchored up there.

What are fireflies and how do they glow in the dark?

Fireflies are not flies at all. During the day the firefly is a dull, not very pretty, slow-moving beetle. But by night, that same beetle glows. Male fireflies flash on and off to signal to females that they're looking for a mate. Some females flash their lights to attract males – both to mate with and eat! Amazingly, although there are more than 100 different types of fireflies in North America, each type has its own special "Morse code." This means that a female never makes the mistake of eating a male from her own group. How does a firefly make light? Chemicals in a special "light organ" below its abdomen combine with oxygen that the firefly breathes in.

Where do flies go in the winter?

Flies spend the winter in a variety of ways, depending on the type. The average adult housefly often sleeps through winter in a building. You may notice flies falling from the rafters in your school gym in February or March. These flies have spent the winter there, hidden away from the cold, but as spring begins to warm things up they become more active. When you haven't eaten for a long time, you sometimes feel groggy, which is just how the flies feel when they wake up.

Other flies spend the winter as eggs laid in garbage or in the rotting carcasses of animals or other insects. These eggs remain safe and warm over the winter and begin to hatch in spring. Still other flies hatch maggotlike larval forms and spend the winter burrowing in soil, plant tissue or garbage until they change into adult flies when the air begins to warm up in spring.

41

Why do bees gather pollen?

Even bees know that to survive they have to eat properly. To grow, young bees need a lot of protein-rich pollen, tiny particles on a plant that help it reproduce. During one summer, an average hive will get all its protein from the almost 45 kg/100 pounds of pollen collected and stored in the hive. And that pollen, combined with honey made from flowers' nectar, gives the bees a well-balanced diet.

How much does a beehive weigh?

On the average, 5,500 bees weigh approximately 500 g/ 1 pound. An active hive in spring may have roughly 25,000 bees in it plus several pounds of stored honey. In the middle to late summer, when the hive is at its most active, it could contain 75,000 bees plus up to 77 kg/170 pounds of honey and so weigh as much as a large man.

Why do bees sting?

Only females sting and they do it to protect themselves. Alas for the female honeybee – she can only sting once and then she dies. When her stinger gets stuck in her enemy, the fishooklike barbs on the end catch hold, causing the stinger, sac and muscles all to break off when the bee pulls away. This leaves a leak in her system, causing her to dry up and die only a few hours later.

Female bumblebees, wasps and hornets are luckier. Because they don't have the barbs to break off, they can keep on stinging.

If you are stung by a bee, don't try to pull out the stinger with your fingers. If you do, you'll end up pinching the poison sac and causing more venom to go into you. Use a pair of tweezers to pry out the entire stinger, or scrape it off with your fingernail. Some people have allergies to bee stings. If someone you know feels nauseous, finds it difficult to breathe or breaks out in hives after a bee sting, make sure he or she gets medical attention immediately.

How many bees are there in a hive and how do they make honey?

In a thriving honeybee hive or colony there can be up to 75,000 bees and all have specific roles to play. The queen, whose role is to lay the eggs, is the "mother" of the hive; then there are 400 to 500 drones, or male honeybees, whose role is to mate with the queen. The rest of the bees – workers, which are undeveloped females – spend their time fetching pollen and nectar to make honey to feed the bees in the hive.

Once worker bees are about three weeks old, they're ready to leave the hive to search for nectar. When they find a field of flowers or a big flowering bush, they fly back to the hive to perform a dance that tells the other workers the exact location of this source of food. Then many more workers fly off, if help is needed, to harvest the nectar and collect pollen.

Throughout the summer, worker bees make several trips to each flower they find. There they suck up the thin, liquid nectar, which they swallow and carry to the hive in their "crop," a thin-walled, baglike, elastic "honey stomach" in their abdomen. When its crop is full, a bee returns to the hive. While the bee is flying, the nectar is partially processed into honey in the crop. When the worker arrives home, she places a tiny drop of nectar into several of the comb's hexagonal waxen cells. The drones finish the processing, fanning the wax with their wings to help evaporate a little of the liquid. The final result is honey.

What's the difference between honey and nectar?

Nectar is a raw material gathered from flowers. Honey is the product that honeybees manufacture from nectar. And in this way bees are more clever than humans. We can make many foods artificially, but we've never figured out how to make honey.

43

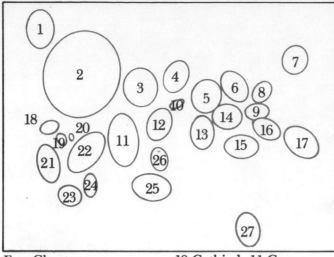

Egg Chart

Index

Picture Credits

pp. 4-5 Hans Reinhard/ Bruce Coleman Inc. 6-7 Ray Boudreau. 8-9 Hans Reinhard/ Bruce Coleman Inc. 10-11 Olena Kassian. 12-13 Fred Bruemmer (walrus); Ted Walker/ Animals Animals (whale spouting); Lynn M. Stone/Animals Animals (domestic hog); Tom McHugh/Photo Researchers, Inc. (stingray); Michael and Barbara Reed/Animals Animals (Pekinese); Peter Swan (caribou); Olena Kassian (camel). 14-15 Wolfgang Bayer/ Bruce Coleman Inc.

(background diver); William H. Amos/Bruce Coleman Inc. (jellyfish); Harry Hartman/Bruce Coleman Inc. (shells); Jane Burton/Bruce Coleman Inc. (female seahorse); Tom McHugh/Photo Researchers, Inc. (electric eel); Ron and Valerie Taylor/Bruce Coleman Inc. (oyster); Kjell B. Sandved/Bruce Coleman Inc. (starfish). 16-17 Tina Holdcroft. 18-19 M.P.L. Fogden/ Bruce Coleman Inc. 20-21, 22-23, 24-25 Olena Kassian. 26-27, 28-29 Joe Weissmann. 30-31 Arthur Holbrook/Miller Services Limited. 32-33, 34-35 Lynda Cooper. 36-37 Tony Thomas. 38-39 Tina Holdcroft. 40-41 Julian Mulock. 42-43 Kim Taylor/Bruce Coleman Inc.

Front Cover: Akira Uchiyama/Photo Researchers, Inc. (Japanese Macaque). Back Cover: Stefen Meyes/Animals Animals

Consultants

J. F. Alex, Department of Environmental Biology, University of Guelph; Roy Anderson, Department of Zoology, University of Guelph; Allan Baker, Department of Ornithology, Royal Ontario Museum; Ian Barker, Department of Pathology, Ontario Veterinary College, University of Guelph; Peter Beamish, Ceta-Research; John Burton, Department of Animal and Poultry Science, University of Guelph; Terry Dickinson; James Eckenwalder, Department of Botany, University of Toronto; John Grayson, Department of Physiology, Faculty of Medicine, University of Toronto; Peter Hallett, Department of Physiology, Faculty of Medicine, University of Toronto; R. Herst, Red Cross Blood Transfusion Clinic; Ross James, Department of Ornithology, Royal Ontario Museum; Finn Larsen, Vancouver Public Aquarium; Ross MacCulloch, Department of Ichthyology and Herpetology, Royal Ontario Museum; Brian Marshall, Department of Entomology, Royal Ontario Museum; Angus McKinnon, Department of Clinical Studies, University of Guelph; Arlene Reiss, Department of Vertebrate Palaeontology, Royal Ontario Museum; Victor Springer, Smithsonian Institution; Thomas Swatland, Department of Animal and Poultry Science, University of Guelph.